Table of Contents

GOD'S
PRESCRIPTION FOR

DIVINE HEALTH

GLORIA COPELAND

HARRISON HOUSE
Tulsa, Oklahoma

God's Prescription for Divine Health

KC • 986 • 1
ISBN 1-88114-986-1
30-0540

© 1995 Kenneth Copeland Publications

Seventh Printing

All scripture is from the *King James Version*
unless otherwise noted.

Published by Harrison House, Inc.
P. O. Box 35035
Tulsa, Oklahoma 74153

Chapter 1

God's Prescription for Divine Health

There is a medicine so powerful it can cure every sickness and disease known to man. It has no dangerous side effects. It is safe even in massive doses. And when taken daily according to directions, it can prevent illness altogether and keep you in vibrant health.

Does that sound too good to be true? It's not. I can testify to you by the Word of God and by my own experience that such a supernatural medicine exists. Even more important, it is available to you every moment of every day.

You don't have to call your doctor to get it. You don't even have to drive to the pharmacy. All you must do is reach for your Bible, open to Proverbs 4:20-24 and follow the instructions you find there:

My son, attend to my words; incline thine ear unto my sayings. Let them not depart from thine eyes; keep them in the midst of thine heart. For they are life unto those that find them, and health *[Hebrew: medicine]* to all their flesh. Keep thy heart with all diligence; for out of it are the

issues of life. Put away from thee a froward mouth, and perverse lips put far from thee.

As simple as they might sound, those four verses contain the supernatural prescription to divine health. It's a powerful prescription that will work for anyone who will put it to work.

If you have received healing by the laying on of hands, following this prescription will help you maintain that healing. If you have believed for healing, but are experiencing lingering symptoms, it will help you stand strong until you are completely symptom-free. And if you are healthy now, it will help you stay that way—not just for a day or a week, but for the rest of your life!

Powerful Medicine

To understand how this prescription works, you must realize that the Word of God is more than just good information. It actually has Life in it. As Jesus said in John 6:63, *"It is the spirit that quickeneth [or makes alive]; the flesh profiteth nothing: the words that I speak unto you, they are spirit, and they are life."*

Every time you take the Word into your heart, believe it and act on it, that Life of which Jesus spoke, the very LIFE of God Himself, is released in you. You may have read the healing scriptures over and over again. You may know them as well as you know your own name. Yet every time you read them or hear them preached, they bring you a fresh dose of God's healing power. Each time, they bring life to you and deliver God's medicine to your flesh.

That's because the Word is like a seed. Hebrews 4:12 says it is *"alive and full of power—making it active, operative, energizing and effective" (The Amplified Bible)*. It actually carries within it the power to fulfill itself.

When you planted the Word about the new birth in your heart, then believed and acted on it, that Word released within you the power to be born again. By the same token, when you plant the Word about healing in your heart, believe and act on it, that Word will release God's healing power in you.

In Isaiah 55:10-11, the Lord describes the process this way:

For as the rain cometh down, and the snow from heaven, and returneth not thither, but watereth the earth, and maketh it bring forth and bud, that it may give seed to the sower, and bread to the eater: So shall my word be that goeth forth out of my mouth: it shall not return unto me void, but it shall accomplish that which I please, and it shall prosper in the thing whereto I sent it.

Add to that the promise of God in Jeremiah 1:12 where He says, *"...I am alert and active, watching over My word to perform it" (The Amplified Bible),* and you can be certain God's Word is powerful medicine you can count on to produce results every time.

Chapter 2

Before Your Eyes and in Your Ears

"But, Gloria," you may say, "I've met people who know the Bible from cover to cover and still can't get healed!"

No doubt you do. But if you'll look back at God's prescription, you'll find it doesn't say anything about "knowing" the Bible. It says *attend* to the Word.

When you attend to something, you give your attention to it. You make it top priority. You set aside other things so you can focus on it. When a nurse is attending to a patient, she looks after him constantly. She doesn't just leave him lying alone in his hospital room while she goes shopping. If someone asks her about her patient, she doesn't feel it's sufficient to say, "Oh, yes. I know him."

In the same way, if you're attending to the Word, you won't leave it lying unopened on the coffee table all day. You won't spend your day focusing your attention on other things.

On the contrary, you'll do what Proverbs 4 says to do. You'll continually incline your ear to God's Word.

Inclining your ear includes more than just putting your physical ears in a position to hear the Word being preached (although that, in itself, is very important). It also means opening the ears of your understanding by meditating and pondering that Word. To truly hear, you must listen with the ears of your spirit to what the Holy Spirit is saying to you through the written Word. Mark 4:23-24 *(The Amplified Bible)* puts it this way:

> **If any man has ears to hear, let him be listening, and perceive and comprehend...Be careful what you are hearing. The measure [of thought and study] you give [to the truth you hear] will be the measure [of virtue and**

knowledge] that comes back to you, and more [besides] will be given to you who hear.

The hearing referred to in those verses is not a passive activity. It requires you to actively engage with God's Word, to believe it and obey it.

In fact, *The Amplified Bible* translates Proverbs 4:20, this way: *"My son, attend to my words; consent and submit to my sayings."* Submitting to the Word means making adjustments in your life. Say, for example, you hear the Word in Philippians 4:4 that you are to *"rejoice in the Lord always."* If you've been doing a lot of griping and complaining, you'll have to change in order to submit to that Word. You'll have to repent and alter your behavior.

In addition to inclining your ear to the Word of God, the Proverbs 4 prescription also says you must keep it before your eyes and not let it depart from your sight. In Matthew 6:22-23, Jesus reveals why that's so important. He says:

The light of the body is the eye: if therefore thine eye be single, thy whole body shall be full of light. But if thine eye be evil, thy whole body shall be full of darkness. If therefore the light that is in thee be darkness, how great is that darkness!

Your eyes are the gateway to your body. If your eye (or your attention) is on the darkness, or the sickness that is in your body, there will be no light to expel it. If, however, the eyes of your heart are trained strictly on the Word, your whole body will eventually be filled with light, and healing will be the result.

I can tell you from experience how important it is to keep the Word constantly before your eyes and in your ears. Several times since I have been walking by faith, I've let myself get too busy to do it. And, almost before I realized it, I became too sick to stay on my feet.

On those occasions, I would immediately get my Bible and begin meditating on the healing scriptures. I would even go to sleep listening to tapes of the Word. Usually, within a few hours, I was completely healed.

There were a few times when I had to stand in faith longer. But whether my healing came instantly or over time, the wonderful truth is—it always came. God's medicine has never failed to bring a healing and a cure in my body.

Take as Directed

Granted, it isn't easy to keep your attention centered on the Word like that. It takes real effort and commitment. It may require getting up a little earlier in the morning or turning off the television at night. But I urge you to do whatever it takes to take God's medicine exactly as directed.

It won't work any other way!

That really shouldn't be so surprising. After all, we wouldn't expect natural medication to work for us if we didn't take it as prescribed. No rational person would set a bottle of pills on the night stand, leave them there and then expect those pills to produce results in his body. No one would call the doctor and say, "Hey, Doc! These pills don't work. I've carried them with me everywhere I go—I keep them in the car with me, I set them on my desk at work, I even have them next to me when I sleep at night—but I don't feel any better."

That would be ridiculous. Yet, spiritually speaking, some people do it all the time. They cry and pray and beg God to heal them, all the while ignoring the medicine He's provided. (They might take a quick dose on Sunday when they go to church, but the rest of the week they don't take time for the Word at all!)

Why do people who love God and believe the Bible act that way? I think it's because they don't understand how putting the Word in their heart can affect their physical bodies. They don't see how something spiritual can change something natural.

If you'll read the Bible, however, you'll see that spiritual power has been affecting this physical world ever since time began. In fact, it was spiritual power released in the form of God's Word that brought this natural world into existence in the first place. Just look at Genesis 1 and you can see that for yourself. It says:

In the beginning God created the heaven and the earth. And the earth was without form, and void; and darkness was upon the face of the deep. And the spirit of God moved upon the face of the waters. *And God said,* **Let there be light: and there was light...***And God said,* **let there be a firmament...***And God said,* **Let the waters under the heaven be gathered together...***And God said,* **let the earth bring forth...***And God said,* **let there be lights in the firmament of the heaven to divide the day**

from the night...*And God said,* Let the waters bring forth abundantly...*And God said,* Let the earth bring forth the living creature after his kind... *And God said,* Let us make man in our image.

Now, in the light of those scriptures, can you believe that God's Word—the force that originally brought into being everything you can see and touch, including your physical body—is still capable of changing that body today? Of course you can! It makes perfect sense.

John G. Lake says this about divine healing and divine health: "Divine healing is the removal by the power of God of the disease that has come upon the body, but the divine health is to live day by day and hour by hour in touch with God so that the life of God flows into the body, just as the life of God flows into the mind or flows into the spirit" *(John G. Lake—His Life, His Sermons, His Boldness of Faith,* pp. 9-10).

———

Chapter 3

What's in Your Heart?

"I'd have no problem at all believing God's Word would heal me
if He'd spoken to me out loud like
He did in Genesis," you might say.
"But He hasn't!"

No, and He probably won't either.
God no longer has to thunder His
Word down at us from heaven.
These days He lives in the hearts of
believers, so He speaks to us from
the inside instead of the outside.
What's more, when it comes to

covenant issues like healing, we don't even have to wait on Him to speak.

He has already spoken!

He has already said, *"By [Jesus'] stripes ye were healed"* (1 Peter 2:24). He has already said, *"I am the Lord that healeth thee"* (Exodus 15:26). He has already said, *"the prayer of faith shall save the sick, and the Lord will raise him up"* (James 5:15).

God has already done His part. So we must do ours. We must take the Word He has spoken, put it inside us and let it change us from the inside out.

You see, everything (including healing) starts inside you. Your future is literally stored up in your heart. As

Jesus said, *"A good man out of the good treasure of the heart bringeth forth good things: and an evil man out of the evil treasure bringeth forth evil things"* (Matthew 12:35).

That means if you want external conditions to be better tomorrow, you'd better start changing your internal condition today. You'd better start taking the Word of God and depositing it in your heart just like you deposit money in the bank. Then you can make withdrawals on it whenever you need it. When sickness attacks your body, you can tap into the healing Word you've put inside you and run that sickness off!

The great thing about your heart account is that, unlike your bank account, there's no limit to the amount you can put into it. You might run out of money to deposit, but you'll never run out of Word. You can put in as much as you want.

Of course, it takes time to make those deposits, but you're the one who decides how much time you're going to spend in the Word. It's strictly up to you!

Some people are hesitant to spend great amounts of time putting the Word about healing in their heart because they think their investment might not pay off. They think they might make sacrifices to attend to the Word and end up sick anyway. But Galatians 6:7-9 puts such concerns to rest. It says:

Be not deceived; God is not mocked: for whatsoever a man soweth, that shall he also reap. For he that soweth to his flesh shall of the flesh reap corruption; but he that soweth to the Spirit shall of the Spirit reap life everlasting. And let us not be weary in well doing: for in due season we shall reap, if we faint not.

It's the unchangeable law of God. Whatever you sow is what you will reap. If you sow cotton, you won't reap peanuts. If you sow cotton, you won't reap doughnuts. And if you steadfastly sow the Word of Life into the soil of your heart, you won't end up with sickness and death. You'll end up with a harvest of divine health. *The New Testament in Modern English* by J. B. Phillips says, "A man's harvest in life will depend entirely on what he sows" (Galatians 6:7).

Keep Your Fountain Flowing

Actually, the Life of God in your heart will not only heal you when you get sick, if that Life abides in you fully, but it will continually keep you in divine health. The Proverbs 4 prescription for healing says it this way: *"Keep thy heart with all diligence; **for out of it are the issues of life"*** (verse 23).

What are the issues or forces of life that flow out of your heart when you're feeding on the Word and fellowshiping with God? They are things like love, joy, peace, longsuffering, gentleness, goodness, faith, meekness and temperance (see Galatians 5:22-23). The Bible calls those forces the fruit of the Spirit. They are the LIFE of God flowing from your heart in abundance. You'll find it is as hard for you to get sick as it used to be for you to get healed. The devil might try to bring sickness on you, but he won't be able to make it stick.

Years ago, the Lord showed me an illustration of that principle I'll never forget. I was in the Philippines, preparing to preach in a meeting at the time and I'd been studying the fruit of the Spirit. As I looked out the window of my hotel room, the Lord brought to my attention a fountain in the courtyard below. He pointed out to me that as long as water was flowing from that fountain, no trash could remain in the mouth of it. Someone might toss some trash in, but the force of the water would just push it right back out again.

I realized then that our hearts are like that fountain. As long as the forces of God's Spirit are flowing out of it, we'll be free from the devil's junk!

How can we make sure those forces keep flowing from our hearts? We must watch over them with all diligence. When we're tempted to get into bitterness or unforgiveness, we must refuse that temptation and yield to love, joy, patience and the other fruit of the Spirit instead. Then we must turn the water of Life up higher by (you guessed it!) turning our attention back to the Word.

Remember this: The forces of life and power coming out of your heart will be in direct proportion to the amount of Word that goes into you.

———◆———

Chapter 4

Faith in Two Places

What happens when your heart gets so full it starts to overflow? Look at Matthew 12:34 and you'll see. It says, *"...out of the abundance of the heart the mouth speaketh."*

So the last step of God's divine prescription is to speak, not words of sickness and disease, discouragement and despair, but words of healing and life, faith and hope. You are to *"Put away from thee a froward mouth, and perverse lips put far from thee*" (Proverbs 4:24). In short, you are to speak the Words of God.

Initially, that may not be easy for you to do. If you're like most people, you've probably spent years talking about how bad things are. At the first sniffle or sneeze, you're likely to say, "I must be catching a cold. I get one every year!" You may not even mean it. But you've spoken like that for so long, it's become habit.

What's more, people are comfortable with that kind of talk. They'll jump right in and say, "Yeah, the same thing happens to me." When you start speaking the Word, however, when you sneeze and say, "I resist you, Cold! I call myself healed, in Jesus' Name! I believe I'm taking healing!"

That will sound so different to other people. That's okay. Talk the Word anyway because for faith to work it must be in two places—in your heart and in your mouth. *"For with the heart man believeth unto righteousness; and with the mouth confession is made unto salvation"* (Romans 10:10).

Some people say that faith will move mountains. But, the scriptural truth is, faith won't even move a molehill for you unless you release it with the words of your mouth.

The Lord Jesus told us that *"whosoever shall **say** unto this mountain,*

*Be thou removed, and be thou cast into the sea; and shall not doubt in his heart, but shall believe that those things which he **saith** shall come to pass; he shall have whatsoever he **saith**"* (Mark 11:23). Notice the word *say* appears three times in that verse while the word *believe* appears only once. Obviously, Jesus wanted us to know that our words are crucial.

It's also important to note that He did not instruct us to talk *about* the mountain, He instructed us to talk *to* it! If we're going to obey Him, we must talk to the mountain of sickness and cast it out of our lives. The Lord told Charles Capps, "I have told My people, they can have what they say, but they are saying what they have!" Instead of saying I'm healed most Christians say, "I'm sick" and reinforce the sickness or disease.

I know one minister who went to visit a young man in the hospital years ago. The fellow was unconscious and had been given up by the doctors to die. As the minister was leaving the hospital room, the Lord spoke to him and told him to let the young man's wife know that her husband would be healed if she would obey Mark 11:23.

So obey it she did! Day after day, she sat next to her unconscious husband and said, "My husband will live and not die in Jesus' Name...My husband will live and not die in Jesus' Name." As a result, that young man was fully healed.

Be Like Abraham

"But, Gloria, it bothers me to say I'm healed when my body still feels sick!"

It shouldn't. It didn't bother Abraham. He went around calling himself the Father of Nations for years even though he was as childless as could be. Why did he do it? Because *"he believed...God, who quickeneth the dead, and calleth those things which be not as though they were"* (Romans 4:17). He was *"fully persuaded that, what [God] had promised, he was able also to perform"* (verse 21).

You see, Abraham wasn't "trying" to believe God. He wasn't just mentally assenting to it. He had immersed himself in God's Word until that Word was more real to him than the things he could see. It didn't matter to him that he was 100 years old. It didn't matter to him that Sarah was far past the age of child-bearing and that she had been barren all her life. All that mattered to him was what God said because he knew His Word was true.

If you don't have that kind of faith for healing right now, then stay in the Word until you get it! After all, *"faith cometh by hearing, and hearing by the word of God"* (Romans 10:17). Read, study, meditate, listen to tapes and watch videos of good, faith-filled teaching, watch our weekly and daily television broadcast EVERY DAY until God's Word about healing is more real to you than the symptoms in your body. Keep on keeping on until, like Abraham, you stagger not at the promise of God through unbelief, but grow strong in faith as you give praise and glory to God (Romans 4:20, *The Amplified Bible*).

Notice that last phrase there doesn't say you give praise to God *because* you're strong in faith. It says you grow strong in faith *as* you give praise to Him. I like that particular translation because I've found it's true. Praising God for your healing is one of the most powerful things you can do.

In fact, Psalm 103 *commands* us to do it. It says, *"Bless the Lord, O my soul: and all that is within me, bless his holy name. Bless the Lord, O my soul, and forget not all his benefits: Who forgiveth all thine iniquities; who healeth all thy diseases"* (verses 1-3).

Chapter 5

———◆◆◆———

Having Done All ...Stand!

As you put God's prescription for health to work in your life, don't be discouraged if you don't see immediate results. Although many times healing comes instantly, there are also times when it takes place more gradually.

So don't let lingering symptoms cause you to doubt. After all, when you go to the doctor, you don't always feel better right away. The medication he gives you often takes some time before it begins to work. But you don't allow the delay to discourage you. You just follow the doctor's orders and expect to feel better soon. Really you are "treating" your spirit that is the source of supernatural life and health for your physical body.

Release that same kind of confidence in God's medicine. Realize that the moment you begin to take it, the healing process begins. Keep your expectancy high and make up your mind to continue standing on the Word until you can see and feel the total physical effects of God's healing power.

When the devil whispers words of doubt and unbelief to you, when he suggests that the Word is not working, deal with those thoughts immediately. Cast them down (see 2 Corinthians 10:5). Speak out loud if necessary and say, "Devil, I rebuke you. I bind you from my mind. I will not believe your lies. God has sent His Word to heal me, and His Word never fails. That Word went to work in my body the instant I believed it, so as far as I am concerned, my days of sickness are over. I declare that Jesus bore my sickness, weakness and pain and I am forever free."

Then, having done all to stand, stand until your healing is fully manifested (see Ephesians 6:12-14). Steadfastly hold your ground. Don't waver. For as James 1:6-8 says, *"he that wavereth is like a wave of the sea driven with the wind and tossed...let not that man think that he shall receive any thing of the Lord. A double minded man is unstable in all his ways."*

If your condition is serious, you may also have to resist the temptation to worry. The devil will try to use anxiety over your situation to choke the Word in your heart and make it unfruitful (Mark 4:19), but don't let him succeed. Just trust God, *"casting all your care upon him; for he careth for you"* (1 Peter 5:7) and constantly keep in mind these wonderful words from Hebrews:

...He Who promised is reliable (sure) and faithful to His word...Do not, therefore, fling

away your fearless confidence, for it carries a great and glorious compensation of reward. For you have need of steadfast patience and endurance, so that you may perform and fully accomplish the will of God, and thus receive and carry away [and enjoy to the full] what is promised (Hebrews 10:23, 35-36, *The Amplified Bible*).

Above all, keep your attention trained on the Word—not on lingering symptoms. Be like Abraham who *"considered not his own body"* (Romans 4:19). Instead of focusing on your circumstances, focus on what God has said to you. Develop an inner image of yourself with your healing fully manifested. See yourself well. See yourself whole. See yourself healed in every way.

Since what you keep before your eyes and in your ears determines what you will believe in your heart and what you will act on, make the Word your number one priority. Attend to it—and it will attend to you!

Healing Scriptures

The following scriptures have helped me get healed, and stay healed, again and again. Read them continually to keep your faith for healing high. Most of them originated from Dodie Osteen, who was healed of terminal liver cancer many years ago. She took them daily like medicine, until every symptom was gone, and still takes them every day to maintain divine health.

To be spoken by mouth three times a day until faith comes, then once a day to maintain faith. If circumstances grow worse, double the dosage. There are no harmful side effects.

—*Charles Capps*

Exodus 15:26

If thou wilt diligently hearken to the voice of the Lord thy God, and wilt do that which is right in his sight, and wilt give ear to his commandments, and keep all his statutes, I will put none of these diseases upon thee, which I have brought upon the Egyptians: for I am the Lord that healeth thee.

Exodus 23:25-26

And ye shall serve the Lord your God, and he shall bless thy bread, and thy water; and I will take sickness away from the midst of thee. There shall nothing cast their young, nor be barren, in thy land: the number of thy days I will fulfil.

Deuteronomy 7:14-15

Thou shalt be blessed above all people: there shall not be male or female barren among you, or among your cattle. And the Lord will take away from thee all sickness, and will put none of the evil diseases of Egypt, which thou knowest, upon thee; but will lay them upon all them that hate thee.

Deuteronomy 30:19-20

I call heaven and earth to record this day against you, that I have set before you life and death, blessing and cursing: therefore choose life, that both thou and thy seed may live: That thou mayest love the Lord thy God, and that thou mayest obey his voice, and that thou mayest cleave unto him: for he is thy life, and the length of thy days: that thou mayest dwell in the land which the Lord sware unto thy fathers, to Abraham, to Isaac, and to Jacob, to give them.

1 Kings 8:56

Blessed be the Lord, that hath given rest unto his people Israel, according to all that he promised: there hath not failed one word of all his good promise, which he promised by the hand of Moses his servant.

Psalm 91:9-10, 14-16

Because thou hast made the Lord, which is my refuge, even the most High, thy habitation; there shall no evil befall thee, neither shall any plague come nigh thy dwelling.

Because he hath set his love upon me, therefore will I deliver him: I will set him on high, because he hath known my name. He shall call upon me, and I will answer him: I will be with him in trouble; I will deliver him, and honour him. With long life will I satisfy him, and show him my salvation.

Psalm 103:1-5

Bless the Lord, O my soul: and all that is within me, bless his holy name. Bless the Lord, O my soul, and forget not all his benefits: Who forgiveth all thine iniquities; who healeth all thy diseases; Who redeemeth thy life from destruction; who crowneth thee with lovingkindness and tender mercies; Who satisfieth thy mouth with good things; so that thy youth is renewed like the eagle's.

Psalm 107:17, 19-21

Fools because of their transgression, and because of their iniquities, are afflicted.

Then they cry unto the Lord in their trouble, and he saveth them out of their distresses. He sent his word, and healed them, and delivered them from their destructions. Oh that men would praise the Lord for his goodness, and for his wonderful works to the children of men!

Psalm 118:17

I shall not die, but live, and declare the works of the Lord.

Proverbs 4:20-24

My son, attend to my words; incline thine ear unto my sayings. Let them not depart from thine eyes; keep them in the midst of thine heart. For they are life unto those that find them, and health to all their flesh. Keep thy heart with all diligence; for out of it are the issues of life. Put away from thee a froward mouth, and perverse lips put far from thee.

Isaiah 41:10

Fear thou not; for I am with thee: be not dismayed; for I am thy God: I will strengthen thee; yea, I will help thee; yea, I will uphold thee with the right hand of my righteousness.

Isaiah 53:4-5

Surely he hath borne our griefs, and carried our sorrows: yet we did esteem him stricken, smitten of God, and afflicted. But he was wounded for our transgressions, he was bruised for our iniquities: the chastisement of our peace was upon him; and with his stripes we are healed.

Jeremiah 1:12

Then said the Lord unto me, Thou hast well seen: for I will hasten my word to perform it.

Jeremiah 17:14

Heal me, O Lord, and I shall be healed; save me, and I shall be saved: for thou art my praise.

Jeremiah 30:17

For I will restore health unto thee, and I will heal thee of thy wounds, saith the Lord.

Joel 3:10

Beat your plowshares into swords, and your pruning hooks into spears: let the weak say, I am strong.

Nahum 1:9

What do ye imagine against the Lord? he will make an utter end: affliction shall not rise up the second time.

Matthew 8:2-3

And, behold, there came a leper and worshipped him, saying, Lord, if thou wilt, thou canst make me clean. And Jesus put forth his hand, and touched him, saying, I will; be thou clean. And immediately his leprosy was cleansed.

Matthew 8:16-17

When the even was come, they brought unto him many that were possessed with devils: and he cast out the spirits with his word, and healed all that were sick: That it might be fulfilled which was spoken by Esaias the prophet, saying, Himself took our infirmities, and bare our sicknesses.

Matthew 15:30-31

And great multitudes came unto him, having with them those that were lame, blind, dumb, maimed, and many others, and cast them down at Jesus' feet; and he healed them: Insomuch that the multitude wondered, when they saw the dumb to speak, the maimed to be whole, the lame to walk, and the blind to see: and they glorified the God of Israel.

Matthew 18:18-19

Verily I say unto you, Whatsoever ye shall bind on earth shall be bound in heaven: and whatsoever ye shall loose on earth shall be loosed in heaven. Again I say unto you, That if two of you shall agree on earth as touching any thing that they shall ask, it shall be done for them of my Father which is in heaven.

Matthew 21:21-22

Jesus answered and said unto them, Verily I say unto you, If ye have faith, and doubt not, ye shall not only do this which is done to the fig tree, but also if ye shall say unto this mountain, Be thou removed, and be thou cast into the sea; it shall be done. And all things, whatsoever ye shall ask in prayer, believing, ye shall receive.

Mark 11:22-24

And Jesus answering saith unto them, Have faith in God. For verily I say unto you, That whosoever shall say unto this mountain, Be thou removed, and be thou cast into the sea; and shall not doubt in his heart, but shall believe that those things which he saith shall come to pass; he shall have whatsoever he saith. Therefore I say unto you, What things soever ye desire, when ye pray, believe that ye receive them, and ye shall have them.

Mark 16:14-18

Afterward he appeared unto the eleven as they sat at meat, and upbraided them with their unbelief and hardness of heart, because they believed not them which had seen him after he was risen. And he said unto them, Go ye into all the world, and preach the gospel to every creature. He that believeth and is baptized shall be saved; but he that believeth not shall be damned. And these signs shall follow them that believe; In my name shall they cast out devils; they shall speak with new tongues; They shall take up serpents; and if they drink any deadly thing, it shall not hurt them; they shall lay hands on the sick, and they shall recover.

Luke 6:19

And the whole multitude sought to touch him: for there went virtue out of him, and healed them all.

Luke 9:2

And he sent them to preach the kingdom of God, and to heal the sick.

Luke 13:16

And ought not this woman, being a daughter of Abraham, whom Satan hath bound, lo, these eighteen years, be loosed from this bond on the sabbath day?

Acts 5:16

There came also a multitude out of the cities round about unto Jerusalem, bringing sick folks, and them which were vexed with unclean spirits: and they were healed every one.

Acts 10:38

How God anointed Jesus of Nazareth with the Holy Ghost and with power: who went about doing good, and healing all that were oppressed of the devil; for God was with him.

Romans 4:16-21

Therefore it is of faith, that it might
be by grace; to the end the promise
might be sure to all the seed; not to
that only which is of the law, but to
that also which is of the faith of
Abraham; who is the father of us all,
(As it is written, I have made thee a
father of many nations,) before him
whom he believed, even God, who
quickeneth the dead, and calleth
those things which be not as though
they were. Who against hope
believed in hope, that he might
become the father of many nations,
according to that which was spoken, So shall thy seed be. And being
not weak in faith, he considered not
his own body now dead, when he

was about an hundred years old, neither yet the deadness of Sarah's womb: He staggered not at the promise of God through unbelief; but was strong in faith, giving glory to God; And being fully persuaded that, what he had promised, he was able also to perform.

Romans 8:2, 11

For the law of the Spirit of life in Christ Jesus hath made me free from the law of sin and death.

But if the Spirit of him that raised up Jesus from the dead dwell in you, he that raised up Christ from the dead shall also quicken your mortal bodies by his Spirit that dwelleth in you.

2 Corinthians 10:3-5

For though we walk in the flesh, we do not war after the flesh: (For the weapons of our warfare are not carnal, but mighty through God to the pulling down of strong holds;) Casting down imaginations, and every high thing that exalteth itself against the knowledge of God, and bringing into captivity every thought to the obedience of Christ.

Galatians 3:13-14, 29

Christ hath redeemed us from the curse of the law, being made a curse for us: for it is written, Cursed is every one that hangeth on a tree: That the blessing of Abraham might come on the Gentiles through Jesus Christ; that we might receive the promise of the Spirit through faith.

And if ye be Christ's, then are ye Abraham's seed, and heirs according to the promise.

Ephesians 6:10-17

Finally, my brethren, be strong in the Lord, and in the power of his might. Put on the whole armour of God, that ye may be able to stand against the wiles of the devil. For we wrestle not against flesh and blood, but against principalities, against powers, against the rulers of the darkness of this world, against spiritual wickedness in high places. Wherefore take unto you the whole armour of God, that ye may be able to withstand in the evil day, and having done all, to stand. Stand therefore, having your loins girt about with truth, and having on the breastplate of right-eousness; And your feet shod with the preparation of the gospel of peace; Above all, taking the shield of faith, wherewith ye shall be able to quench all the fiery darts of the wicked. And take the helmet of sal-vation, and the sword of the Spirit, which is the word of God.

Philippians 2:13

[Not in your own strength] for it is God Who is all the while effectually at work in you—energizing and creating in you the power and desire—both to will and to work for His good pleasure and satisfaction and delight *(The Amplified Bible).*

Philippians 4:6-9

Do not fret or have any anxiety about anything, but in every circumstance and in everything by prayer and petition [definite requests] with thanksgiving continue to make your wants known to God. And God's peace [be yours, that tranquil state of a soul assured of its salvation through Christ, and so fearing nothing from God and content with its earthly lot of whatever sort that is, that peace] which transcends all understanding, shall garrison and mount guard over your hearts and minds in Christ Jesus. For the rest, brethren, whatever is true, whatever is worthy of reverence and is honorable and seemly, whatever is just, whatever is pure, whatever is lovely and lovable, whatever is kind and winsome and gracious, if there is any virtue and excellence, if there is anything worthy of praise, think on and weigh and take account of these things—fix your minds on them. Practice what you have learned and received and heard and seen in me, and model your way of living on it, and the God of peace—of untroubled, undisturbed well-being—will be with you *(The Amplified Bible)*.

2 Timothy 1:7

For God hath not given us the spirit of fear; but of power, and of love, and of a sound mind.

Hebrews 10:23

Let us hold fast the profession of our faith without wavering; (for he is faithful that promised).

Hebrews 10:35-36

Cast not away therefore your confidence, which hath great recompence of reward. For ye have need of patience, that, after ye have done the will of God, ye might receive the promise.

Hebrews 11:11

Through faith also Sarah herself received strength to conceive seed, and was delivered of a child when she was past age, because she judged him faithful who had promised.

Hebrews 13:8

Jesus Christ the same yesterday, and today, and for ever.

James 4:7

Submit yourselves therefore to God. Resist the devil, and he will flee from you.

James 5:14-16

Is any sick among you? let him call for the elders of the church; and let them pray over him, anointing him with oil in the name of the Lord: And the prayer of faith shall save the sick, and the Lord shall raise him up; and if he have committed sins, they shall be forgiven him. Confess your faults one to another, and pray one for another, that ye may be healed. The effectual fervent prayer of a righteous man availeth much.

1 Peter 2:24

Who his own self bare our sins in his own body on the tree, that we, being dead to sins, should live unto righteousness: by whose stripes ye were healed.

1 John 3:21-22

Beloved, if our heart condemn us not, then have we confidence toward God. And whatsoever we ask, we receive of him, because we keep his commandments, and do those things that are pleasing in his sight.

1 John 5:14-15

And this is the confidence that we have in him, that, if we ask any thing according to his will, he heareth us: And if we know that he hear us, whatsoever we ask, we know that we have the petitions that we desired of him.

3 John 2

Beloved, I wish above all things that thou mayest prosper and be in health, even as thy soul prospereth.

Revelation 12:11

And they overcame him by the blood of the Lamb, and by the word of their testimony; and they loved not their lives unto the death.

Prayer for Salvation and Baptism in the Holy Spirit

Heavenly Father, I come to You in the Name of Jesus. Your Word says, *"Whosoever shall call on the name of the Lord shall be saved"* (Acts 2:21). I am calling on You. I pray and ask Jesus to come into my heart and be Lord over my life, according to Romans 10:9-10: *"If thou shalt confess with thy mouth the Lord Jesus, and shalt believe in thine heart that God hath raised him from the dead, thou shalt be saved. For with the heart man believeth unto righteousness; and with the mouth confession is made unto salvation."* I do that now. I confess that Jesus is Lord, and I believe in my heart that God raised Him from the dead.

I am now reborn! I am a Christian—a child of Almighty God! I am saved! You also said in Your Word, *"If ye then, being evil, know how to give good gifts unto your children: HOW MUCH MORE shall your heavenly Father give the Holy Spirit to them that ask him?"* (Luke 11:13). I'm also asking You to fill me with the Holy Spirit. Holy Spirit, rise up within me as I praise God. I fully expect to speak with other tongues as You give me utterance (Acts 2:4).

Begin to praise God for filling you with the Holy Spirit. Speak those words and syllables you receive—not in your own language, but the language given to you by the Holy Spirit. You have to use your own voice. God will not force you to speak. Worship and praise Him in your heavenly language—in other tongues.

Continue with the blessing God has given you and pray in tongues each day.

You are a born-again, Spirit-filled believer. You'll never be the same!

Find a good Word of God preaching church, and become a part of a church family who will love and care for you as you love and care for them.

We need to be hooked up to each other. It increases our strength in God. It's God's plan for us.

About the Author

Together with her husband, Kenneth, Gloria Copeland's impact on the kingdom of God has been felt worldwide. She teaches around the world on God's will for healing and divine health, His plan for prosperity, His great plan for man's salvation and more. With an anointing for powerful preaching and the compassion of Jesus for the sick, Gloria moves and ministers in the Spirit of God. Recipient of the Christian Woman of the Year Award, her book Hidden Treasures was recently number 16 on the Christian Booksellers Association bestseller list.

Books Available from
Kenneth Copeland Ministries

by Kenneth Copeland
* A Ceremony of Marriage
  A Matter of Choice
  Covenant of Blood
  Faith and Patience—The Power Twins
* Freedom From Fear
  Giving and Receiving
  Honor—Walking in Honesty, Truth and Integrity
  How to Conquer Strife
  How to Discipline Your Flesh
  How to Receive Communion
  Living at the End of Time—A Time of Supernatural Increase
  Love Never Fails
  Managing God's Mutual Funds
* Now Are We in Christ Jesus
* Our Covenant With God
* Prayer—Your Foundation for Success
  Prosperity: The Choice Is Yours
  Rumors of War
* Sensitivity of Heart
  Six Steps to Excellence in Ministry
  Sorrow Not! Winning Over Grief and Sorrow
* The Decision Is Yours
* The Force of Faith
* The Force of Righteousness
  The Image of God in You
  The Laws of Prosperity
* The Mercy of God
  The Miraculous Realm of God's Love
  The Outpouring of the Spirit—The Result of Prayer
* The Power of the Tongue
  The Power to Be Forever Free
  The Troublemaker
* The Winning Attitude
  Turn Your Hurts Into Harvests
* Welcome to the Family
* You Are Healed!
  Your Right-Standing With God

by Gloria Copeland
* And Jesus Healed Them All
  Are You Ready?
  Build Your Financial Foundation
  Build Yourself an Ark
  Fight On!
  God's Prescription for Divine Health
  God's Success Formula
  God's Will for You
  God's Will for Your Healing
  God's Will is Prosperity
* God's Will Is the Holy Spirit
* Harvest of Health
  Hidden Treasures
  Living Contact
* Love—The Secret to Your Success
  No Deposit—No Return

Pleasing the Father
Pressing In—It's Worth It All
Shine On!
The Power to Live a New Life
The Unbeatable Spirit of Faith
* Walk in the Spirit
Walk With God
Well Worth the Wait

Books Co-Authored by Kenneth and Gloria Copeland
Family Promises
Healing Promises
Prosperity Promises
Protection Promises

From Faith to Faith—A Daily Guide to Victory
From Faith to Faith—A Perpetual Calendar

One Word From God Series
• One Word from God Can Change Your Destiny
• One Word from God Can Change Your Family
• One Word from God Can Change Your Finances
• One Word from God Can Change Your Formula for Success
• One Word from God Can Change Your Health
• One Word from God Can Change Your Nation
• One Word from God Can Change Your Prayer Life
• One Word from God Can Change Your Relationships

Over the Edge—A Youth Devotional
Over the Edge Xtreme Planner for Students—
    Designed for the School Year

Pursuit of His Presence—A Daily Devotional
Pursuit of His Presence—A Perpetual Calendar

Other Books Published by KCP
The First 30 Years—A Journey of Faith
    The story of the lives of Kenneth and Gloria Copeland
Real People. Real Needs. Real Victories.
    A book of testimonies to encourage your faith.

John G. Lake—His Life, His Sermons, His Boldness of Faith
The Holiest of All, by Andrew Murray
The New Testament in Modern Speech,
  by Richard Francis Weymouth

Products Designed for Today's Children and Youth
Baby Praise Board Book
Baby Praise Christmas Board Book
Noah's Ark Coloring Book
Shout! Super-Activity Book

Commander Kellie and the Superkids Adventure Novels
#1   Escape from Jungle Island
#2   In Pursuit of the Enemy
#3   Mysterious Presence, The
#4   Quest for the Second Half, The

SWORD Adventure Book

*Available in Spanish

World Offices
of Kenneth Copeland Ministries

For more information and a free catalog, please
write the office nearest you.

Kenneth Copeland Ministries
Fort Worth, Texas 76192-0001

Kenneth Copeland
Locked Bag 2600
Mansfield Delivery Centre
QUEENSLAND 4122
AUSTRALIA

Kenneth Copeland
Post Office Box 15
BATH
BA1 1GD
ENGLAND U.K.

Kenneth Copeland
Private Bag X 909
FONTAINEBLEAU 2032
REPUBLIC OF SOUTH AFRICA

Kenneth Copeland
Post Office Box 378
SURREY, BC V3T 5B6
CANADA

UKRAINE
L'VIV 290000
Post Office Box 84
Kenneth Copeland
L'VIV 290000
UKRAINE

Learn more about Kenneth Copeland Ministries
by visiting our website at:
www.kcm.org

To receive a FREE subscription to *Believer's Voice of Victory*, or to give a child you know a FREE subscription to *Shout!*, write:

Kenneth Copeland Ministries
Fort Worth, Texas 76192-0001
or call:
1-800-600-7395
(9 a.m.-5 p.m. CT)
Or visit our website at:
www.kcm.org

If you are writing from outside the U.S., please contact the KCM office nearest you. Addresses for all Kenneth Copeland Ministries offices are listed on the previous page.

WE'RE HERE FOR YOU!

Believer's Voice of Victory Television Broadcast

Join Kenneth and Gloria Copeland, and the *Believer's Voice of Victory* broadcasts Monday through Friday and on Sunday each week, and learn how faith in God's Word can take your life from ordinary to extraordinary. This teaching from God's Word is designed to get you where you want to be—*on top!*

You can catch the *Believer's Voice of Victory* broadcast on your local, cable or satellite channels.

*Check your local listings for times
and stations in your area.

Believer's Voice of Victory Magazine

Enjoy inspired teaching and encouragement from Kenneth and Gloria Copeland and guest ministers each month in the *Believer's Voice of Victory* magazine. Also included are real-life testimonies of God's miraculous power and divine intervention into the lives of people just like you!

It's more than just a magazine—it's a ministry.

Shout! . . . The dynamic magazine for kids!

Shout! The Voice of Victory for Kids is a Bible-charged, action-packed, bimonthly magazine available FREE to kids everywhere! Featuring Wichita Slim and Commander Kellie and the Superkids, *Shout!* is filled with colorful adventure comics, challenging games and puzzles, exciting short stories, solve-it-yourself mysteries and much more!!

Stand up, sign up and get ready to *Shout!*

The Harrison House Vision

Proclaiming the truth and the power
Of the Gospel of Jesus Christ
With excellence;

Challenging Christians to
Live victoriously,
Grow spiritually,
Know God intimately.